May all yo
And may t
surprises a
delights.
May the celebrations begin with
happiness and end in quiet
contentment.

_To:_ Dear To-

From: Maureen
with love &
fondest good wishes,
for the coming
year ahead
God Bless you
in 1996.

XX

There is a gentleness, a healing at this time of year.
We wait together for the end of cold and darkness. Each of us different - yet united in our dream of love and hope and kindness.

PAM BROWN. b.1928

This is the heart of darkness, when all mankind since time began has feared that spring may never come. Touch hands. We are none of us alone. Heap up the fires, celebrate - and wait in hope for spring.

CHARLOTTE GRAY, b.1928

Though the sky be gloomy, the
hedge bare, and the trees gaunt,
yet among the bushes a solitary
green leaf has already put forth.
It is ... the first in the new year -
in the very darkest and blackest
days - to show that life is stirring.

RICHARD JEFFERIES (1848-1887)

In the depth of winter, when nature lies despoiled of every charm and wrapped in her shroud of sheeted snow, we turn for our gratifications to moral sources ... we draw our pleasures from the deep wells of living kindness....

WASHINGTON IRVING (1783-1859)

There is something in the very
season of the year that gives a
charm to the festivity.... Our
thoughts are more concentrated;
our friendly sympathies more
aroused. We feel more sensibly
the charm of each other's society,
and are brought more closely

together by dependence on each
other for enjoyment.

WASHINGTON IRVING (1783–1859)

Such a winter eve. Now for a
mellow fire, some old poet's page,
or else serene philosphy.

HENRY DAVID THOREAU (1817–1862)

W. F. Choults

For a moment we forget the drab
formalities. We decorate our
winter world, light up the
darkened streets - call greetings,
smile, reach out our hands to
friends and strangers.
Let it not be ephemeral, this
warmth, this joy, this kindness.

PAM BROWN, b.1928

To you who celebrate this holiday in sunlight, in the scent of flowers, in the sound of tropical seas - I wish you a dream of snow.

Of candlelight and curtains drawn against the winter dark.

PAM BROWN. b.1928

Peace and love and joy can
bloom like flowers in the snow.
Or in the jungle's heat.
Or in the drab city streets.
Or in the desert's loneliness.
Wherever men and women wish
each other well.

PETER GRAY, b.1928

Where does the honest face of hospitality expand into a broader and more cordial smile than by the winter fireside? Amid the general call to happiness, the bustle of the spirits, and stir of affections, which prevail at this period, what bosom can remain insensible?

WASHINGTON IRVING (1783-1859)

The dreariness and desolation of the landscape, the short and gloomy days and darksome nights ... shut in our feelings also from rambling abroad, and make us more kindly disposed for the pleasure of the social circle.

WASHINGTON IRVING (1783-1859)

I hope for snow - white and clean and glittering in the winter sunlight, covering all that's left of the year that's gone. A new beginning. A gentle stillness. A new life that will bring us joy and peace.

PAM BROWN, b.1928

To see a hillside white with dogwood bloom is to know a particular ecstasy of beauty, but to walk the gray Winter woods and find the buds which will resurrect that beauty in another May is to partake of continuity.

HAL BORLAND

There was nothing very cheerful in the climate or the town, and yet there was an air of cheerfulness abroad that the clearest summer air and brightest summer sun might have endeavoured for in vain.

CHARLES DICKENS (1812-1870)

And what do I want for you
in the New Year?
Peace of mind,
The joy of living and seeing,
The medicine of laughter,
The key to lock out fear,
And to walk, my dear,
Through the days of life -
- With me.

CATHERINE COOKSON, b.1906,
from *Let Me Make Myself Plain*

Be at war with your vices, at
peace with your neighbors, and
let every New Year find you a
better man.

BENJAMIN FRANKLIN (1706-1790)

Villagers all, this frosty tide,
Let your doors swing open wide,
Though wind may follow, and
snow beside,
Yet draw us in by your fire to
bide;
Joy shall be yours in the
morning!

KENNETH GRAHAME (1859-1932)

This is a time for healing. The year is almost over. Let it go. Today is a new beginning. It's a time to learn from our mistakes, forgive ourselves, throw away any bitterness and move toward the spring.

PAM BROWN, b.1928